Life in Ancient Rome

Carmel Reilly

NELSON
CENGAGE Learning™

Australia • Brazil • Japan • Korea • Mexico • Singapore • Spain • United Kingdom • United States

Life in Ancient Rome

Text: Carmel Reilly
Editor: Rebecca Crisp
Design: Karen Mayo
Series design: James Lowe
Photo researcher: Lisa Piemonte
Production controllers: Renee Cusmano and Lisa Porter
Reprint: Siew Han Ong

Acknowledgements
The author and publisher would like to acknowledge permission to reproduce material from the following sources:
Corbis Australia: pp. 8, 21 (top), 22, 23; Dorling Kindersley: p. 9; Jupiterimages Corporation © 2009: p. 7; Photolibrary: pp. 1, 3, 6, 10, 12, 14, 15, 16, 17 (both), 21 (bottom), cover, back cover; Richard Morden © Cengage Learning Australia: pp. 4–5; Virginia Gray © Cengage Learning Australia: pp. 11, 13, 18, 19, 20.

Every effort has been made to trace and acknowledge copyright. However, if any infringement has occurred, the publishers tender their apologies and invite the copyright holders to contact them.

Fast Forward Independent Texts
Level 19

For product information and technology assistance,
in Australia call 1300 790 853;
in New Zealand call 0508 635 766

For permission to use material from this text or product,
please email **aust.permissions@cengage.com**

ISBN 978 0 17 017948 5
ISBN 978 0 17 017898 3 (set)

Cengage Learning Australia
Level 7, 80 Dorcas Street
South Melbourne, Victoria Australia 3205

Cengage Learning New Zealand
Unit 4B Rosedale Office Park
331 Rosedale Road, Albany, North Shore NZ 0632

For learning solutions, visit **cengage.com.au**

Printed in Australia by Ligare Pty Ltd
3 4 5 22 21 20

Life in Ancient Rome

Carmel Reilly

Contents

The First Great Superpower

Ancient Rome became one of the biggest **empires** in history.
It was the world's first great **superpower**.

In the beginning,
the ancient Romans controlled only the city of Rome,
but over time their power grew.

Oceanus Germanicus
Britannia
Germania Inferior
Belgica
Germania Superior
GALLIA
Mare Adriatic
Roma
Corsica
ITAL
Sardinia
Mare Tyrrhenum
Sicilia
HISPANIA
Africa Proconsularis
Oceanus Atlanticus

about 753 BC: rise of ancient Rome

mid-600s BC: expansion of the Roman Empire

800 BC | 700 BC | 600 BC | 500 BC | 400 BC | 300 BC | 200 BC

timeline of ancient Rome

The ancient Romans lived more than 2000 years ago. In the seventh century **BC**, they began taking over nearby **territories**. By about 117 **AD** their empire stretched from England to Asia.

The Roman Empire came to an end in about 450 AD.

Government

In the early days,
ancient Rome was ruled by kings.
But in 509 BC,
the Romans set up a **republic**
with **elected** leaders.
The republic lasted almost 500 years.

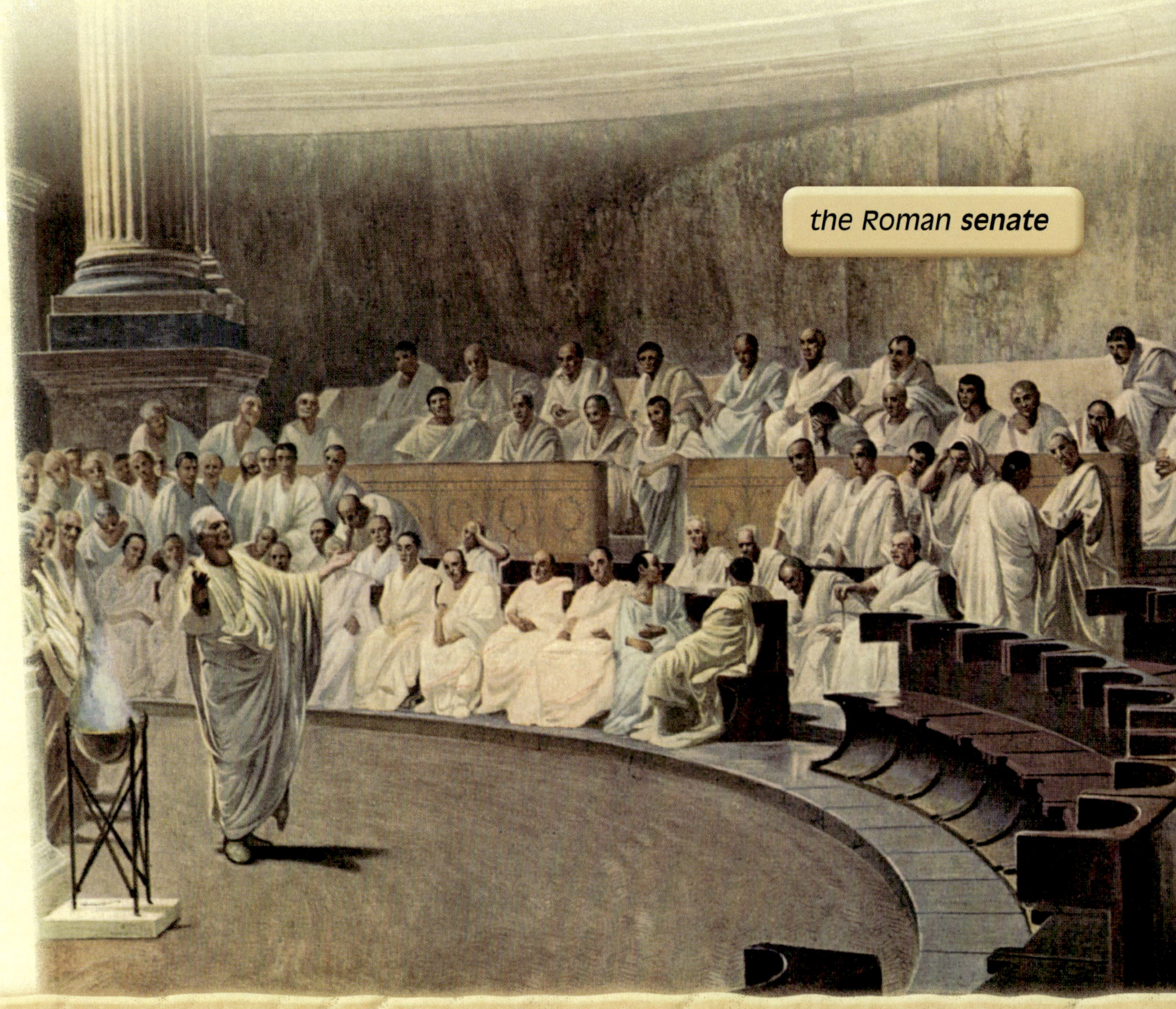

*the Roman **senate***

about 753 BC: rise of ancient Rome

mid-600s BC: expansion of the Roman Empire

509 BC: republic

800 BC | 700 BC | 600 BC | 500 BC | 400 BC | 300 BC | 200 BC

Then in 27 BC,
the republic ended.

The leaders who took control
were not elected
and Roman **citizens** no longer had a say
in how Rome was run.

Julius Caesar helped to end the Roman Republic.

27 BC: end of republic

117 AD: height of the Roman Empire

450 AD: fall of the Roman Empire

00 BC | 0 | 100 AD | 200 AD | 300 AD | 400 AD | 500 AD

CHAPTER 2

Daily Life

There were big differences
in the day-to-day lives
of rich Romans and poor Romans.

Home

Rich Romans lived in large houses
with gardens.
They did not have to work
because they owned **slaves**
who did most of the work for them.

a rich Roman woman and her slaves

In the cities, poor Romans lived in crowded blocks of flats. They worked long hours for little money, and did not always have enough food to eat.

poor Romans at home

Food

Rich Romans enjoyed huge feasts. Many of them owned large farms where they grew crops and kept animals for meat.

They could also afford to buy food from other countries.

Slaves did all their shopping and cooking for them.

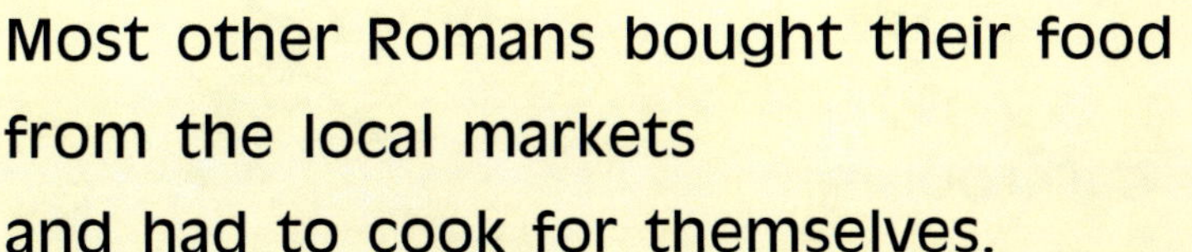

Most other Romans bought their food from the local markets and had to cook for themselves.

Bread, honey, olives, porridge, eggs and fruit were some of the common foods.

Poor people did not have much money and sometimes the only time that they ate was at lunch.

an ancient Roman market

The Baths

Most Romans did not have bathrooms with running water in their homes. They went to public buildings called baths to keep themselves clean.

the ruins of a Roman bath

Every town had public baths
where people could go to wash.
Men and women had separate baths.

People went to the baths not just
to keep clean,
but also to meet up
with their friends.

Work

Some rich Romans were traders or ran small **industries**. They used slaves to do almost all of their work.

Some Romans had jobs as doctors and teachers. Others became builders or soldiers.

ancient Roman builders

Poorer people made goods or food, or ran small shops in the markets.

Slaves could not choose what they wanted to do. They had to do what their owners told them to do.

Slaves had to work for little or no payments.

Free Time

The Romans liked to keep fit
and took part in many different types of sports.
They watched horse-racing,
and all kinds of fighting.
They watched animals fighting each other,
men fighting each other
and animals fighting men.

Many Romans were also interested in design and the arts. They built beautiful homes and gardens.

They liked to watch plays, listen to music, read and write, and discuss ideas.

ancient Roman musicians

CHAPTER 3

Children

In ancient Rome,
most children from poorer families
did not go to school.
They learned a trade
from their fathers or mothers,
or worked in the markets for other people.

a Roman boy learning to make ceramic pots

Many boys, and some girls,
from richer families went to school.
Some families had a teacher
who came to their home.

Rich children often went to school.

Trade

The Romans were great traders.
They built ships that could carry goods
to and from many other parts
of the empire.

They also traded goods with people
from other places,
such as Asia and Africa.

Some of the goods that the Romans sent to other countries were pottery, glass and olive oil.

ancient Roman glass objects

jars used to store olive oil

Roman traders brought back things such as dried fruit and fabrics.

War

War was a big part of Roman life. Many Romans became soldiers. Soldiers led an exciting life, with the chance to travel and live in faraway places.

The Romans went to war
to protect parts of their empire
or to take over new areas.

Success in war was what made the Roman Empire grow into the world's first superpower.

Glossary

AD	"anno domini"; refers to any year after the birth of Jesus Christ
BC	"before Christ"; refers to any year before the birth of Jesus Christ
citizens	people who live in a particular city or country
elected	chosen by the people
empires	groups of countries or regions ruled by a single government
industries	large-scale business activities
republic	a country whose leaders do not inherit power, but are elected by some or all of the people
senate	the governing council of ancient Rome
slaves	people owned by other people and forced to work for little or no payment
superpower	a very powerful country
territories	areas of land

Index